Cooking For Cookbook

Healthy And Delicious Recipes For Two Recipes

Table of Contents

Introduction

This cookbook features a great variety of healthy and tasty recipes for two. It can be hard finding recipes for only two people. I always used to toss out half of my meals that I cooked simply because me and my partner were unable to finish the leftovers of recipes I made. The recipes in this cookbook solved this problem for me, and I want to share them.

These are handpicked healthy recipes for two from my collection. These recipes are great for serving two people and if you are looking for healthy recipes for two, then you will surely love this cookbook!

Chapter 1: Healthy Breakfast Recipes For Two

Quinoa Porridge

Ingredients

1/3 cup quinoa

1/8 teaspoon ground cinnamon

1 cup almond milk

1/3 cup water

1 tablespoon agave syrup

3/4 teaspoon vanilla extract (optional)

pinch salt

Directions

Heat a saucepan over medium heat and measure in the quinoa. Season with cinnamon and cook until toasted, stirring frequently, about 3 minutes. Pour in the almond milk, water and vanilla and stir in the brown sugar and salt.

Bring to a boil, then cook over low heat until the porridge is thick and grains are tender, about 25 minutes.

Add more water if needed if the liquid has dried up before it finishes cooking. Stir occasionally.

Blueberry Whole Wheat Pancakes

Ingredients

1 1/4 cups whole wheat flour

2 teaspoons baking powder

1 egg

1 cup milk, plus more if necessary

1/2 teaspoon salt

1 tablespoon artificial sweetener

1/2 cup blueberries

Directions

Sift together flour and baking powder, set aside. Beat together the egg, milk, salt and artificial sweetener in a bowl. Stir in flour until just moistened, add blueberries, and stir to incorporate.

Preheat a heavy-bottomed skillet over medium heat, and spray with cooking spray. Pour approximately 1/4 cup of the batter into the pan for each pancake. Cook until bubbly, about 1 1/2 minutes. T

Turn, and continue cooking until golden brown.

4

Almond Banana Oatmeal

Ingredients

2 small bananas

2 cups almond milk

2 tablespoons honey

2 teaspoons almond extract

1/2 teaspoon ground cinnamon, or more to taste

2 pinches salt

1 cup rolled oats

Directions

Mash half the banana in a saucepan. Whisk almond milk, honey, almond extract, cinnamon, and salt with the mashed banana until smooth; bring to a boil and stir oats into the mixture.

Reduce heat to medium-low and cook at a simmer until the oats are tender and the moisture has been absorbed to your desired consistency, 5 to 7 minutes. Transfer oatmeal to a bowl.

Dice remaining banana half. Top oatmeal with banana and more cinnamon, as desired.

Tofu Breakfast Burritos

Ingredients

1 teaspoon extra-virgin olive oil

1 cup crumbled extra-firm tofu

2 tablespoons fresh salsa

Pinch of freshly ground pepper

2 tablespoons shredded Monterey Jack cheese

2 whole-wheat tortillas

Pinch of salt

Directions

Heat oil in a small nonstick skillet over medium-high heat. Add tofu and cook, stirring occasionally, until beginning to brown, about 2 minutes.

Stir in salsa, salt and pepper; continue cooking until heated through, about 30 seconds.

Spread cheese down the center of tortilla. Top with the tofu mixture. Fold in the ends of the tortilla and roll into a burrito.

Egg White Omelet For Two

Ingredients

1 tablespoon chopped onion

1 tablespoon chopped green bell pepper

1 tablespoon chopped mushrooms

salt and ground black pepper to taste

1/2 (32 ounce) container refrigerated pasteurized egg white substitute

Directions

Spray a 9x5-inch glass or microwave-safe loaf pan with cooking spray; sprinkle the onion, green bell pepper, and mushrooms into the pan, and toss lightly with a fork just to mix. Season with salt and black pepper, and pour in the egg whites.

Cook in a microwave oven on High setting for 3 minutes. Remove and stir the cooked egg white from the side of the pan into the rest of the ingredients; cook for 3 more minutes on High; Turn over and microwave for 30 more seconds on High. Adjust salt and pepper, and serve.

Coconut Oatmeal

Ingredients

1 cup and 3 tablespoons plain or vanilla soy milk

1/8 teaspoon salt

2/3 cup rolled oats

1 tablespoon pure maple syrup

2 tablespoons raisins

2 tablespoons dried cranberries

1 tablespoon sweetened flaked coconut

2 tablespoons chopped walnuts

1/3 (8 ounce) container plain yogurt (optional)

1 tablespoon honey

Directions

Pour the milk and salt into a saucepan, and bring to a boil. Stir in the oats, maple syrup, raisins, and cranberries. Return to a boil, then reduce heat to medium. Cook for 5 minutes.

Stir in walnuts and coconut, and let stand until it reaches your desired thickness. Spoon into serving bowls, and top with yogurt and honey, if desired.

Pumpkin Porridge

Ingredients

1 cup quick-cooking rolled oats

3/4 cup milk, or as needed

1/2 cup canned pumpkin puree

1/4 teaspoon pumpkin pie spice

1 teaspoon cinnamon sugar

Directions

Mix together oats and milk in a microwave-safe bowl. Cook on high for 1 to 2 minutes, stirring once. Add more milk or oats to achieve the desired consistency, and cook for another 30 seconds.

Stir in pumpkin puree, pumpkin pie spice, and cinnamon sugar. Heat through, and serve.

Spinach Energy Breakfast Smoothie

Ingredients

4 cups fresh spinach

2 cup almond milk

2 tablespoon peanut butter

2 tablespoon chia seeds (optional)

2 leaf kale

2 sliced frozen banana

Directions

Blend spinach, almond milk, peanut butter, chia seeds, and kale together in a blender until smooth. Add banana and blend until smooth.

Cinnamon Apple Oatmeal

Ingredients

1 cup water

1/4 cup apple juice

1 apple, cored and chopped

2/3 cup rolled oats

1 teaspoon ground cinnamon

1 cup milk

Directions

Combine the water, apple juice, and apples in a saucepan. Bring to a boil over high heat, and stir in the rolled oats and cinnamon. Return to a boil, then reduce heat to low, and simmer until thick, about 3 minutes.

Spoon into serving bowls, and pour milk over the servings.

Yogurt Berry Breakfast Bowl

Ingredients

1 cup nonfat plain Greek yogurt

3½ ounces frozen pure unsweetened acai fruit puree (see Tip)

1 cup frozen blueberries

1 frozen medium banana

3/4 cup coconut water

2 tablespoons fresh raspberries

2 tablespoons granola

2 teaspoons toasted unsweetened coconut flakes

1 teaspoon chia seeds

Directions

Combine yogurt, acai, blueberries, banana and coconut water in a blender. Puree until smooth.

Pour smoothie into a bowl and top with raspberries, granola, coconut and chia seeds.

Whole Grain Oatmeal Pancakes

Ingredients

2 tablespoons whole wheat flour

2 tablespoons all-purpose flour

2 tablespoons rolled oats

2 tablespoons cornmeal

1 teaspoon granular no-calorie sucralose sweetener

1/4 teaspoon salt

1/2 teaspoon baking powder

1/4 teaspoon baking soda

1/4 teaspoon ground cinnamon

1 egg whites

1 tablespoon plain non fat yogurt

1 tablespoon skim milk

1 tablespoon water

Directions

In a medium bowl, stir together the whole wheat flour, all-purpose flour, oats, cornmeal, sweetener, salt, baking powder, baking soda and cinnamon. In a separate bowl, whisk together the eggs, yogurt, milk and water. Pour the wet ingredients into the dry, and mix just until moistened.

Heat a skillet over medium heat, and coat with cooking spray. Pour about 1/3 cup of batter per pancake onto the skillet. Cook until bubbles begin to form in the center, then flip and cook until browned on the other side.

Cherry Oatmeal Breakfast Smoothie

Ingredients

½ cup water

⅓ cup quick-cooking rolled oats

½ cup light almond milk or fat-free milk

¾ cup fresh or frozen unsweetened strawberries, partially thawed

½ cup fresh or frozen unsweetened pitted dark sweet cherries, partially thawed

1 to 2 tablespoons almond butter

1 tablespoon honey

½ cup small ice cubes

Directions

In a medium bowl combine water and oats. Microwave 1 minute. Stir in ¼ cup of the milk. Microwave 30 to 50 seconds more or until oats are very tender. Cool 5 minutes.

In a blender combine oat mixture, the remaining ¼ cup milk, and the next four ingredients (through honey). Cover and blend until smooth, scraping container as needed.

16

Add ice cubes; cover and blend until smooth. If desired, top each serving with additional fruit.

Almond Chia Porridge With Blueberries

Ingredients

½ cup unsweetened almond milk

2 tablespoons chia seeds

2 teaspoons pure maple syrup

⅛ teaspoon almond extract

½ cup fresh blueberries, divided

1 tablespoon toasted slivered almonds, divided

Directions

Stir together almond milk, chia, maple syrup and almond extract in a small bowl. Cover and refrigerate for at least 8 hours.

When ready to serve, stir the pudding well. Spoon about half the pudding into a serving glass and top with half the blueberries and almonds.

Add the rest of the pudding and top with the remaining blueberries and almonds.

Vegetable Tofu Scramble

Ingredients

1½ teaspoons extra-virgin olive oil

5 ounces extra-firm tofu, drained and cubed

1 cup chopped vegetables, such as zucchini, mushrooms and onions

1/2 teaspoon spice of choice, such as chili powder or ground cumin

1/2 cup canned chickpeas, rinsed

1/3 cup salsa

1/2 cup shredded Cheddar cheese

Hot sauce and chopped cilantro to taste

Pinch of ground pepper

Directions

Heat oil in a large nonstick skillet over medium-high heat. Add tofu, vegetables, spice and pepper; cook, stirring often, until the vegetables are softened, 5 to 7 minutes.

Add chickpeas and salsa and heat through, 1 to 2 minutes.

Remove from heat, gather the scramble into one section of the pan, top with Cheddar cheese and let melt off the heat. Serve with hot sauce and cilantro, if desired.

Cinnamon Apple Quinoa Bowl

Ingredients

1 cup low-fat milk

⅔ cup diced apple, divided

1/2 cup quinoa

¼ teaspoon ground cinnamon

⅛ teaspoon salt

4 teaspoons sliced almonds

½ teaspoon agave nectar

Directions

Combine milk, 1/3 cup apple, quinoa, cinnamon and salt in a small saucepan. Bring to a boil.

Cover and simmer on very low heat until the liquid is absorbed, about 12 minutes.

Let stand 5 minutes. Top with the remaining apple, almonds and agave.

Tangy Banana Breakfast Smoothie

Ingredients

1 cup cold milk

2 oranges, peeled and segmented

1 banana

1/4 cup sugar (or sugar substitute)

1 pinch salt

1/2 (8 ounce) container vanilla fat-free yogurt

4 cubes ice

Directions

In a blender, combine milk, oranges, banana, sugar, salt and yogurt. Blend for about 1 minute. Insert ice cubes, and blend until smooth. Pour into glasses and serve.

Orange Cinnamon Oatmeal

Ingredients

1.5 cups old-fashioned rolled oats

1 teaspoon ground cinnamon, or to taste

1/2 cup dried cranberries

1 cup frozen blueberries

1/2 teaspoon ground turmeric (optional)

2 pinches ground ginger (optional)

2 cups water

1/2 cup orange juice, or as needed

Directions

Place the rolled oats, cinnamon, cranberries, and blueberries in a microwave safe bowl. Add the turmeric and ginger, if desired. Pour in the water, and stir to mix ingredients.

Cook on High until water is absorbed, about 2 minutes. Stir in orange juice to desired consistency.

Breakfast Hash For Two

Ingredients

1 tablespoon olive oil

1/2 sweet potato, peeled and cut into ¾-inch pieces

1/4 cup chopped onion

½ cup refrigerated, cooked crumbled turkey sausage

3/4 cup liquid egg substitute

½ teaspoon dried Italian seasoning, crushed

¼ teaspoon garlic powder

¼ teaspoon black pepper

⅛ teaspoon salt

1 cup fresh baby spinach

½ cup shredded reduced-fat 4-cheese blend

Directions

Heat a 10-inch cast iron skillet over medium heat. Add oil to skillet. Add sweet potato; cook 15 minutes, stirring occasionally.

Add onion and sausage. Cook 5 minutes more or until vegetables are tender, stirring frequently.

Add the egg product, Italian seasoning, garlic powder, pepper, and salt. Cook, without stirring, until mixture begins to set on bottom and around edges.

Using a spatula or large spoon, lift and fold partially cooked egg mixture so uncooked portion flows underneath.

Continue cooking 2 to 3 minutes or until egg substitute is cooked through but still moist. Gradually add spinach, tossing just until wilted. Sprinkle with cheese.

Chapter 2: Healthy Lunch Recipes For Two

Mediterranean Bean Salad

Ingredients

1/4 (15 ounce) can cannellini (white kidney) beans, rinsed and drained

1/4 (15 ounce) can garbanzo beans, rinsed and drained

1/4 (15 ounce) can dark red kidney beans, rinsed and drained

1/8 onion, minced

1/2 clove garlic, minced

1-1/2 teaspoons minced fresh parsley, or to taste

1 tablespoon olive oil

1/4 lemon, juiced

salt and ground black pepper to taste

Directions

Combine cannellini beans, garbanzo beans, kidney beans in a mixing bowl. Add onion, garlic, parsley, olive oil, lemon juice, salt, and black pepper; mix well.

Creamy Butternut Soup

Ingredients

1/2 cup corn

1.5 teaspoons olive oil

1/2 clove garlic, minced

1/2 onion, chopped

1/2 butternut squash, peeled and cubed

1-1/2 cups vegetable stock

1/2 teaspoon dried basil

1/4 teaspoon ground black pepper

1/4 cup plain yogurt

1/4 teaspoon ground nutmeg

Directions

Heat the olive oil in a Dutch oven over medium-high heat. Cook and stir the garlic and onion in the oil until soft and translucent. Add the butternut squash and corn and cook for 3 more minutes. Pour the stock into the Dutch oven and bring to a boil; season with basil and black pepper.

Reduce the heat to medium-low and simmer uncovered until the squash is tender, about 15 minutes. Remove the Dutch oven from the heat and using a hand blender, or working in batches with a counter top blender, process the soup until smooth. Stir in the yogurt and nutmeg.

Barley And Tomato Soup

Ingredient

1/3 cup chopped onions

1/3 cup chopped celery

1/3 cup chopped carrots

3/4 teaspoon minced garlic

2 teaspoons vegetable oil

1 cup water

1 tomato, diced

1/2 can peeled and diced tomatoes with juice

1/2 can chicken broth

1/4 cup uncooked barley

1/2 teaspoon ground black pepper

Directions

In a large saucepan over medium heat, combine the onions, celery, carrots, garlic and oil and saute for 5 to 10 minutes, or until all vegetables are almost tender.

Then add the water, fresh tomatoes, canned tomatoes, chicken broth, barley and ground black pepper.

Stir thoroughly and bring to a boil. Reduce heat to low and simmer for 35 to 40 minutes, or until barley is tender.

Cilantro Quinoa Salad

Ingredients

1/2 cup water

1/3 cup uncooked quinoa, rinsed

1 tablespoon and 1 teaspoon red bell pepper, chopped

1 tablespoon and 1 teaspoon yellow bell pepper, chopped

1/2 small red onion, finely chopped

1/2 teaspoon curry powder

1 tablespoon and 1 teaspoon chopped fresh cilantro

1/2 lime, juiced

2 tablespoons toasted sliced almonds

2.5 tablespoons minced carrots

2.5 tablespoons dried cranberries

salt and ground black pepper to taste

Directions

Pour the water into a saucepan, and cover with a lid. Bring to a boil over high heat, then pour in the quinoa, recover, and continue to simmer over low heat until the water has been absorbed, 15 to 20 minutes. Scrape into a mixing bowl, and chill in the refrigerator until cold.

Once cold, stir in the red bell pepper, yellow bell pepper, red onion, curry powder, cilantro, lime juice, sliced almonds, carrots, and cranberries.

Season to taste with salt and pepper. Chill before serving.

Chicken Pasta Salad

Ingredients

2/3 cup diced cooked chicken

1/4 teaspoon finely chopped, peeled fresh ginger

2 tablespoons rice vinegar

1.5 tablespoons orange juice

1 tablespoon and 1 teaspoon vegetable oil

1/4 teaspoon toasted sesame oil

3/8 package dry onion soup mix

3/4 teaspoon white sugar

3/8 clove garlic, pressed

1/2 package bow tie pasta

1/4 cucumber - scored, halved lengthwise, seeded, and sliced

1/4 cup diced red bell pepper

1/4 cup coarsely chopped red onion

1 diced Roma tomato

1/2 carrot, shredded

1/2 bag fresh spinach

1/2 can mandarin orange segments, drained

2 tablespoons sliced almonds, toasted

Directions

To make the dressing, whisk together the ginger root, rice vinegar, orange juice, vegetable oil, sesame oil, soup mix, sugar, and garlic until well blended. Cover, and refrigerate until needed.

Bring a large pot of lightly salted water to a boil. Add the bowtie pasta and cook for 8 to 10 minutes or until al dente; drain, and rinse under cold water. Place pasta in a large bowl.

To make the salad, toss the cucumber, bell pepper, onion, tomatoes, carrot, spinach, mandarin oranges, chicken, and almonds with the pasta. Pour the dressing over the salad mixture, and toss again to coat evenly. Serve immediately.

Spicy Rice And Corn Salad

Ingredients

1/3 cup and 1 tablespoon cooked brown rice

1/4 can kidney beans, rinsed and drained

1/4 can black beans, rinsed and drained

1/4 can whole kernel corn, drained

1/4 small onion, diced

1/4 green bell pepper, diced

1 jalapeno pepper, seeded and diced

1 lime, zested and juiced

2-1/2 teaspoons chopped cilantro leaves

1/4 teaspoon minced garlic

1/4 teaspoon ground cumin

salt to taste

Directions

In a large salad bowl, combine the brown rice, kidney beans, black beans, corn, onion, green pepper, jalapeno peppers, lime zest and juice, cilantro, garlic, and cumin.

Lightly toss all ingredients to mix well, and sprinkle with salt to taste.

Refrigerate salad for 1 hour, toss again, and serve.

Spicy Carrot Soup

Ingredients

1 red bell peppers, seeded and chopped

1/2 teaspoon extra virgin olive oil

1 carrots, chopped

1/2 yellow onion, chopped

1 celery ribs, chopped

1 clove garlic, chopped

1.5 cups chicken broth

1/3 cup long grain rice

1 teaspoon chopped fresh thyme

1/4 teaspoon cayenne pepper

1/4 teaspoon crushed red pepper flakes

1/2 teaspoon salt

1/2 teaspoon ground black pepper

Directions

Heat the olive oil in a large pot over medium-high heat. Stir in the bell peppers, carrots, onions, celery, and garlic. Cook and stir the vegetables until soft, about 10 minutes.

Stir in the chicken broth, rice, thyme, cayenne pepper, red pepper flakes, salt and pepper, and bring the mixture to a boil. Reduce heat, cover, and simmer until the rice and vegetables are tender, about 25 minutes. Remove from heat. and cool 30 minutes.

Blend the cooled soup until smooth using an hand-held immersion blender directly in the pot.

Or use a blender, and blend the soup in batches until smooth.

Kale And Bean Soup For Two

Ingredients

3/4 teaspoon olive oil or canola oil

2 large garlic cloves, crushed or minced

1/4 medium yellow onion, chopped

1 cup chopped raw kale

1 cup low-fat, low-sodium chicken or vegetable broth

1/2 can white beans, such as cannellini or navy, undrained

1 plum tomatoes, chopped

1/2 teaspoon dried Italian herb seasoning

1/4 cup chopped parsley

Salt and pepper to taste

Directions

In a large pot, heat olive oil. Add garlic and onion; saute until soft. Add kale and saute, stirring, until wilted. Add 3 cups of broth, 2 cups of beans, and all of the tomato, herbs, salt and pepper.

Simmer 5 minutes. In a blender or food processor, mix the remaining beans and broth until smooth. Stir into soup to thicken. Simmer 15 minutes. Ladle into bowls; sprinkle with chopped parsley.

Shrimp And Asparagus Salad For Two

Ingredients

5 ounces fresh asparagus, trimmed and cut into 1 inch pieces

4 extra-large shrimp

1 clove garlic, minced

2 teaspoons extra-virgin olive oil

2.5 cups water

2.5 ounces orzo pasta

2 teaspoons extra-virgin olive oil

1/2 green onion, chopped

1 teaspoon white balsamic vinegar

1 teaspoon fresh lemon juice

3/4 teaspoon honey mustard

2 teaspoons minced fresh basil

salt and pepper to taste

Directions

Peel shrimp, reserving the shells. In a skillet over medium heat, cook the garlic and shrimp in 2 tablespoons of olive oil, stirring frequently to keep the garlic from browning. When shrimp are cooked through, remove from heat, cool and cut into 1/2-inch pieces.

Bring water to a boil in a Dutch oven over high heat. Add shrimp shells, boil for 5 minutes, then strain out shells and discard. Stir in the orzo and cook for 5 minutes. Stir in the asparagus pieces and continue cooking until the pasta is al dente, about 4 minutes. Drain into a mesh sieve, and rinse in cold water.

Toss pasta and asparagus with 2 tablespoons of olive oil, shrimp, and green onions until evenly coated. In a separate bowl, whisk the vinegar, lemon juice, mustard, and basil until incorporated.

Pour over pasta mixture and toss well; season to taste with salt and pepper. Chill for 2 hours.

Cucumber Thai Salad

Ingredients

1 pound cucumbers - halved, seeded, and sliced

2.5 tablespoons distilled white vinegar

2.5 tablespoons white sugar

1/4 teaspoon ground coriander

1/4 teaspoon crushed red pepper flakes

1/4 teaspoon salt

1/4 cup finely chopped red onion

1 roma (plum) tomatoes, chopped

1 tablespoon chopped fresh cilantro

1 tablespoon chopped fresh mint

2 tablespoons chopped roasted peanuts

fresh mint sprigs

Directions

Whisk together the vinegar, sugar, coriander, red pepper flakes, and salt in a salad bowl until the sugar is dissolved. Stir in the cucumbers, onion, tomatoes, cilantro, and chopped mint, and toss to coat with dressing. Cover and refrigerate for 1 hour to blend the flavors.

Before serving, toss again with chopped peanuts, and garnish with sprigs of fresh mint.

Chapter 3: Healthy Main Dish Recipes For Two

Teriyaki Tuna

Ingredients

1 tablespoon light soy sauce

1/2 tablespoon Chinese rice wine

1/2 tablespoon minced fresh ginger root

1/2 large clove garlic, minced

2 tuna steaks

1 tablespoon vegetable oil

Directions

Stir soy sauce, rice wine, ginger, and garlic together in a shallow dish. Place tuna in the marinade, and turn to coat. Cover dish and refrigerate for at least 30 minutes.

Preheat grill for medium-high heat.

Remove tuna from marinade and discard remaining liquid. Brush both sides of steaks with oil.

Cook tuna on the preheated grill until cooked through, 3 to 6 minutes per side.

Lime Avocado Tilapia

Ingredients

1/2 canned chipotle pepper in adobo sauce

1 tablespoon adobo sauce from the can

2 tablespoons salsa

1-1/2 teaspoons lime juice

2 tilapia fillets

1/4 package tortilla chips, crushed

1/2 small avocado - peeled, pitted, and cut into large chunks

2 tablespoons sour cream

1.5 teaspoons lime juice

1 tablespoon and 1.5 teaspoons milk

salt and pepper to taste

Directions

Preheat oven to 375 degrees F (190 degrees C). Grease a baking sheet with cooking spray.

Combine the chipotle pepper, adobo sauce, salsa, and 1 tablespoon lime juice in a blender and blend until smooth; brush the mixture over both sides of each tilapia fillet.

Spread the crushed tortilla chips into the bottom of a deep dish; dredge the coated fillets in the chips to coat. Arrange the fillets on the prepared baking pan.

Bake the fillets 15 minutes; turn and lightly spray with cooking spray. Continue to bake until golden brown, another 10 to 15 minutes.

While the fish bakes, place the avocado, sour cream, and 1 tablespoon lime juice and blend until smooth.

Stir in the milk 1 tablespoon at a time until the consistency is similar to ranch dressing. Season with salt and pepper. Spoon the sauce over the baked fillets to serve.

Rosemary Salmon

Ingredients

1 lemon, thinly sliced

4 sprigs fresh rosemary

2 salmon fillets, bones and skin removed

coarse salt to taste

1 tablespoon olive oil, or as needed

Directions

Preheat oven to 400 F.

Arrange half the lemon slices in a single layer in a baking dish. Layer with 2 sprigs rosemary, and top with salmon fillets. Sprinkle salmon with salt, layer with remaining rosemary sprigs, and top with remaining lemon slices. Drizzle with olive oil.

Bake 20 minutes in the preheated oven, or until fish is easily flaked with a fork.

Garlic Chicken

Ingredients

2 tablespoons olive oil

1 clove garlic, crushed

2 tablespoons Italian-seasoned bread crumbs

2 tablespoons grated Parmesan cheese

2 skinless, boneless chicken breast halves

Directions

Preheat oven to 425F.

Heat olive oil and garlic in a small saucepan over low heat until warmed, 1 to 2 minutes. Transfer garlic and oil to a shallow bowl.

Combine bread crumbs and Parmesan cheese in a separate shallow bowl.

Dip chicken breasts in the olive oil-garlic mixture using tongs; transfer to bread crumb mixture and turn to evenly coat. Transfer coated chicken to a shallow baking dish.

Bake in the preheated oven until no longer pink and juices run clear, 30 to 35 minutes. An instant-read thermometer inserted into the center should read at least 165 degrees F.

Spicy Lime Chicken

Ingredients

1/4 teaspoon salt

1/8 teaspoon black pepper

1/8 teaspoon cayenne pepper

1/8 teaspoon paprika

1/8 teaspoon garlic powder

1/8 teaspoon onion powder

1/8 teaspoon dried thyme

1/8 teaspoon dried parsley

2 boneless, skinless chicken breast halves

1 tablespoon butter

1-1/2 teaspoons olive oil

1 teaspoon garlic powder

1 tablespoon and 1-1/2 teaspoons lime juice

Directions

In a small bowl, mix together salt, black pepper, cayenne, paprika, 1/4 teaspoon garlic powder, onion powder, thyme and parsley. Sprinkle spice mixture generously on both sides of chicken breasts.

Heat butter and olive oil in a large heavy skillet over medium heat. Saute chicken until golden brown, about 6 minutes on each side. Sprinkle with garlic powder and lime juice.

Cook 5 minutes more, stirring frequently to coat evenly with sauce.

Baked Tilapia

Ingredients

2 fillets tilapia

1 teaspoon butter

1/8 teaspoon herb seasoning, or to taste

1/4 teaspoon garlic salt, or to taste

1/2 lemon, sliced

1/2 package frozen cauliflower with broccoli and red pepper

Directions

Preheat the oven to 375 F. Grease a 9x13 inch baking dish.

Place the tilapia fillets in the bottom of the baking dish and dot with butter. Season with Old Bay seasoning and garlic salt. Top each one with a slice or two of lemon. Arrange the frozen mixed vegetables around the fish, and season lightly with salt and pepper.

Cover the dish and bake for 25 to 30 minutes in the preheated oven, until vegetables are tender and fish flakes easily with a fork.

Black Bean Chili

Ingredients

1 teaspoon vegetable oil

1/2 onion, diced

1 clove garlic, minced

5 ounces ground turkey

1 can black beans, undrained

1/2 can crushed tomatoes

1.5 teaspoons chili powder

1 teaspoon dried oregano

1 teaspoon dried basil leaves

1 teaspoon red wine vinegar

Directions

Heat the oil in a large heavy pot over medium heat; cook onion and garlic until onions are translucent. Add turkey and cook, stirring, until meat is brown.

Stir in beans, tomatoes, chili powder, oregano, basil and vinegar. Reduce heat to low, cover and simmer 60 minutes or more, until flavors are well blended.

Balsamic Chicken Thighs

Ingredients

2 bone-in chicken thighs

½ teaspoon salt, divided

¼ teaspoon pepper

1 tablespoon extra-virgin olive oil

1 cup cranberries, thawed if frozen

¼ cup balsamic vinegar

1 tablespoon honey

1 teaspoon chopped fresh thyme, plus more for garnish

Directions

Sprinkle chicken with ¼ teaspoon each salt and pepper. Heat oil in a large skillet over medium-high heat. Add the chicken, skin-side down, reduce heat to medium and cook, undisturbed, until golden brown, about 7 minutes. Remove all but 1 tablespoon fat from the pan.

Turn the chicken over and add cranberries, vinegar, honey and thyme to the pan. Bring to a simmer over high heat, then reduce heat to maintain a simmer.

Partially cover and cook, stirring occasionally, until an instant-read thermometer inserted in the thickest part without touching bone reaches 165°F, 10 to 12 minutes.

Transfer the chicken to a serving platter. Increase heat to high, add the remaining ¼ teaspoon salt and cook uncovered, stirring, until the sauce is thickened, about 1 minute. Serve the chicken with the sauce.

Spicy Cayenne Chicken Breasts For Two

Ingredients

1 tablespoon and 3/4 teaspoon paprika

1 tablespoon garlic powder

1-1/2 teaspoons salt

1-1/2 teaspoons onion powder

1-1/2 teaspoons dried thyme

1-1/2 teaspoons ground cayenne pepper

1-1/2 teaspoons ground black pepper

2 skinless, boneless chicken breast halves

Directions

In a medium bowl, mix together the paprika, garlic powder, salt, onion powder, thyme, cayenne pepper, and ground black pepper. Set aside about 3 tablespoons of this seasoning mixture for the chicken; store the remainder in an airtight container for later use.

Preheat grill for medium-high heat. Rub some of the reserved 3 tablespoons of seasoning onto both sides of the chicken breasts.

Lightly oil the grill grate. Place chicken on the grill, and cook for 6 to 8 minutes on each side, until juices run clear.

Cheesy Chicken Chili

Ingredients

1-1/2 teaspoons olive oil

2 skinless, boneless chicken breast halves - cubed

1/2 onion, chopped

1/2 cup and 2 tablespoons chicken broth

1/2 (4 ounce) can diced green chiles

1/2 teaspoon garlic powder

1/2 teaspoon ground cumin

1/4 teaspoon dried oregano

1/4 teaspoon dried cilantro

1/8 teaspoon cayenne pepper

1/2 (15 ounce) can cannellini beans, drained and rinsed

1 green onions, chopped

1 ounce shredded Monterey Jack cheese

Directions

Heat oil in a large saucepan over medium-high heat. Cook chicken and onion in oil 4 to 5 minutes, or until onion is tender.

Stir in the chicken broth, green chilies, garlic powder, cumin, oregano, cilantro, and cayenne pepper. Reduce heat, and simmer for 15 minutes.

Stir in the beans, and simmer for 5 more minutes, or until chicken is no longer pink and juices run clear. Garnish with green onion and shredded cheese.

Chicken Tortilla Soup

Ingredients

1 cup water

1/2 skinless, boneless chicken breast

1/8 onion, chopped

1/4 can kidney beans

1/4 can ranch-style beans

1/4 can pinto beans

1/4 can black beans, rinsed and drained

1/4 can white hominy

1/2 can diced tomatoes with green chile peppers

1/4 package taco seasoning mix

1/8 (1 ounce) package ranch dressing mix

Directions

Combine the chicken and water in a large pot over high heat. Cook for 30 minutes to 1 hour, or until chicken is done. Remove chicken from the pot, and cut into bite-size pieces.

Return the meat to the pot. Add the onion, kidney beans, ranch style beans, pinto beans, black beans, hominy, tomatoes, taco seasoning and ranch dressing mix.

Mix well, reduce heat to low, and simmer for 30 minutes or until heated through.

Broccoli Stir-Fry

Ingredients

1 large broccoli head

1/2 medium red onion

½ cup water, divided

1 tablespoon rice wine or dry sherry

1 tablespoon reduced-sodium tamari

1 tablespoon chili-garlic sauce

1 teaspoons toasted sesame oil, divided

1 teaspoons cornstarch

1 teaspoon light brown sugar

2 tablespoons peanut oil, divided

⅛ teaspoon salt

1 small red chili, sliced (seeded if desired)

1 tablespoon minced fresh ginger

2 tablespoons chopped roasted unsalted peanuts

Directions

Remove florets from broccoli stems. Cut the florets into 1-inch pieces and set aside. Trim the stem ends. Using a vegetable spiralizer with the thin-noodle blade, spiralize as much of each stem as possible. Chop any remaining stem into ½-inch pieces. Switch to the thick-noodle blade and spiralize onion.

Whisk ¼ cup water, rice wine (or sherry), tamari, chile-garlic sauce, 2 teaspoons sesame oil, cornstarch and brown sugar in a small bowl. Set by the stove.

Heat 1 tablespoon peanut oil in a large flat-bottom carbon-steel wok over medium-high heat. Add the broccoli noodles, stem pieces and onion; cook, stirring, until tender, about 5 minutes.

Transfer the mixture to a large bowl and toss with the remaining 2 teaspoons sesame oil and salt.

Add the remaining 1 tablespoon peanut oil, chilies and ginger to the pan. Cook, stirring constantly, for 15 seconds. Add the reserved florets and cook, stirring, until starting to brown, about 1 minute.

Add the remaining ¼ cup water, cover and cook until the florets are tender, about 3 minutes more. Uncover and add the reserved sauce. Cook, stirring, until the sauce is thick, about 1 minute.

Arrange the noodle mixture on a platter with the florets on top. Serve sprinkled with peanuts.

White Bean Soup

Ingredients

1/2 teaspoon olive oil

1 leeks, bulb only, chopped

1/2 clove garlic, chopped

1/2 (16 ounce) can fat-free chicken broth

1/2 (16 ounce) can cannellini beans, rinsed and drained

1/2 bay leaves

1/2 teaspoon ground cumin

2 tablespoons whole wheat couscous

1/2 cup packed fresh spinach

salt and pepper to taste

Directions

Heat olive oil in a large saucepan or soup pot over medium heat. Add the leeks and garlic; saute until tender, about 5 minutes. Stir in the chicken broth, cannellini beans, bay leaves and cumin.

Bring to a boil, then reduce the heat to low, and stir in the couscous. Cover, and simmer for 5 minutes. Stir in spinach and season with salt and pepper. Serve immediately.

Turkey Squash Chili

Ingredients

1 teaspoon olive oil

1/4 onion, chopped

1 clove garlic, minced

2-1/2 ounces ground turkey breast

2-1/2 ounces butternut squash - peeled, seeded and cut into 1-inch dice

1 tablespoon and 1 teaspoon chicken broth

1/8 can chopped green chilies

1/2 can petite diced tomatoes

1/8 can kidney beans with liquid

1/8 can white hominy, drained

1/8 can tomato sauce

1/2 teaspoon chili powder

1/2 teaspoon ground cumin

1/8 teaspoon garlic salt

Directions

Heat the olive oil in a large pot over medium heat. Stir in the onion and garlic; cook and stir for 3 minutes, then add the turkey, and stir until crumbly and no longer pink.

Add the butternut squash, chicken broth, green chilies, tomatoes, kidney beans, hominy, and tomato sauce; season with chili powder, cumin, and garlic salt.

Bring to a simmer, then reduce heat to medium-low, cover, and simmer until the squash is tender, about 20 minutes.

Chicken And Bell Pepper Stir Fry

Ingredients

2 teaspoons canola oil

1 boneless, skinless chicken breast, trimmed and cut into 1-inch pieces

2 teaspoons ground cumin, divided

½ teaspoon kosher salt, divided

½ cup finely chopped fresh cilantro

1 medium red bell peppers, chopped

3/4 cup sliced carrots

3/4 cup chopped red onion

3 tablespoons water

1 cup rinsed canned hominy

1 clove garlic, minced

1/4 can diced green chilies

2 tablespoons lime juice

1/2 firm ripe avocado, diced

Directions

Heat oil in a large non stick skillet over medium-high heat. Add chicken and sprinkle with 1 teaspoon cumin and ¼ teaspoon salt.

Cook, stirring occasionally, until the chicken is just cooked through, 5 to 7 minutes. Transfer to a bowl and toss with cilantro. Cover to keep warm.

Add bell peppers, carrots, onion, water and the remaining ¼ teaspoon salt to the pan. Cook, stirring often, until the vegetables are crisp-tender, about 5 minutes.

Stir in hominy, garlic and the remaining 2 teaspoons cumin; cook, stirring, for 1 minute. Stir in green chilies and lime juice and cook for 1 minute more.

Serve the chicken over the hominy mixture, topped with avocado.

Sweet Potato Chili

Ingredients

1 tablespoon plus 2 teaspoons extra-virgin olive oil

1/2 medium-large sweet potato, peeled and diced

1/2 large onion, diced

4 cloves garlic, minced

1 tablespoons chili powder

2 teaspoons ground cumin

1/4 teaspoon ground chipotle chili

¼ teaspoon salt

1.5 cups water

1/2 can black beans, rinsed

2/3 can diced tomatoes

2 teaspoons lime juice

1/4 cup chopped fresh cilantro

Directions

Heat oil in a Dutch oven over medium-high heat. Add sweet potato and onion and cook, stirring often, until the onion is beginning to soften, about 4 minutes. Add garlic, chili powder, cumin, chipotle and salt and cook, stirring constantly, for 30 seconds.

Add water and bring to a simmer. Cover, reduce heat to maintain a gentle simmer and cook until the sweet potato is tender, 10 to 12 minutes.

Add beans, tomatoes and lime juice; increase heat to high and return to a simmer, stirring often.

Reduce heat and simmer until slightly reduced, about 5 minutes. Remove from heat and stir in cilantro.

Printed in Poland
by Amazon Fulfillment
Poland Sp. z o.o., Wrocław

55635985R00047